The Agony of Healing

by Adeline Whitmore

<u>Chapter One</u>

The Pain of Breaking

The Pain of Breaking

How foolish of me it was
To give my heart
To someone so careless
So reckless
So disingenuous

And now I'm here
On the kitchen floor
Weeping

This is the pain
Of breaking.

Rumors

I've been hearing
Rumors around town
That you
Have already
Moved on.

I don't know what
Hurts me more;

The way things ended
Or what you've been doing
Since then

Was I so worthless to you
That you moved on
So quickly?

Rumors.

You Laughed When

My heart
Hit the floor
And shattered
Into a thousand pieces

Villain

I don't want to give you
The satisfaction
Of being the villain
In my story

Painful Affliction

The two most painful things
In the world
Are childbirth
And heartbreak

What a shame it is
That women
Are afflicted with both

Turning Tables

Don't try
To turn the tables
On me

I'll keep my distance
From you

Lies.

It was all lies.

Every I love you
Every caress
Every whisper

All of it was fake
And I fell for it all
Like a damned fool

I guess
I can only blame
Myself
For being
Such a fool.

Remember

When
Will I see you
Again?

Oh, ghost of memories
Harbinger of phantom love

The pain of remembering
We're over.

<u>Every Time</u>

I hate the way
I can't stay angry
At you
As much as you deserve

I soften like butter
On the kitchen counter

Every time

Dance In The Flames

Dance in the flames
Embrace the pain

Self-discovery.

<u>Forever & Always</u>

I used to think
You would be my
Forever and always

How could I be
Such a fool?

Every time
I fall
For your pretty lies

Gameplan

Drown my sorrows
In a bottle of wine

Just get through the night
Then fight my way
Through this

So Close, So Far

What a terrible thing it was
To have been
So close
To you

And now
Here we are
So far apart

I wonder
If it would've been better
To have never felt
Your love at all..

No Destination

I drive out of the city
Out onto the highway
No destination in mind
Just needing
To get out
And get my mind
Off of you

Regret.

There's no one like you
And that's the tragedy
To have loved and lost
Someone so perfect
How could I have let
Everything end like this?

Moonlit Sorrow

I stay up at night
Wondering
If you miss me
Like I miss you

Fantasies of Happy Endings

I fantasize about going up
To your doorstep

When you open the door,
I kiss you
Push you on the couch
And make up for everything.

I just can't accept
That it's over.

Addict

My mind
Is addicted to you

I can't keep you
Out of my thoughts
For too long

<u>Him</u>

There's an ocean out there,
I tell myself

You will find
Someone else

But I don't care
I just want
Him

Bittersweet Aftertaste

In my daydreams
We kiss again
But I snap out of it
And taste
This bittersweet aftertaste;

Fond memories
Of passionate love
Tinged with heartbreak.

Hoodies & Heartbreak

I found one of your hoodies
Under my bed today
It still smells like you
And I swear
As I inhale that scent
I can almost pretend
You're still mine.

When I Was With You

It sucks to look outside
At the falling leaves
And remember
How everything
Used to look so much
More beautiful
When I was with you

Desperate For Answers

Looking through old texts
Knowing I shouldn't

Looking for clues and hints
Just desperate for an answer
Why things went wrong

Badly Broken

If I told you
How badly
You broke me

Would you
Even care?

You'll Always Be

You'll always be
That one person
I can never get
Out of my mind
No matter how hard
I try

One Day

One day
I hope
Everything
Will fall
In place

And everything
Will be
Okay

<u>Chapter Two</u>

The Cruelty of Goodbyes

The Cruelty of Goodbyes

The hardest goodbye
Is letting go
Of the way you once felt
For someone
And letting go of dreams
Of rekindling the fire

The hardest goodbye
Is letting go
Of you

Fool

He promised a future
She trusted him

Remember

I only ask
That you remember me
For the good times
And not for the pain

Beautiful

I was beautiful
Before you told me I was
And I'm still beautiful
Now that you don't tell me
Anymore

Waste My Time

I know
You weren't worth
My time

But I'd be lying
If I said
I'd say no
If you asked me
To waste my time
Again

Chasing Glitter

No matter who
You move on with

I'll always know
You lost a diamond
Chasing glitter

Loving

Loving him
Hurt me
Loving myself
Will heal me

Heartbreak

It hurts
Like jagged glass
Slashed across
Your palms

Summertime Happiness

Everything
Used to be
So simple.

I Will Rise

Losing him
Will be the fuel
That propels me
To space

I will rise.

Let In The Light

The hardest part
Of heartbreak
Is not closing down
Not collapsing

Revenge.

I forgot about you
For a moment
Laying in his bed
Caressing his hair

Revenge.

Closure

Don't try to explain
Why it ended
Sometimes
There's no answer

Need

It sucks to need someone
Who doesn't need you back

Hallelujah

Raise me up
With the sound
Of a gospel choir

March

Love is a long, hard march
Across barren countrysides
Looking for moments
Of beauty and light

<u>Feel.</u>

Your feelings
Are valid

Don't let anyone
Tell you otherwise

Truth

You are so beautiful
Don't let anyone
Tell you otherwise

Breakup Songs

The worst part
Of breakups
Is wasting your favorite songs
On people
Who don't deserve them

Look Out For Yourself

If he doesn't make you happy
Just leave him
It's that simple

Sometimes you just have to
Look out for yourself

Love Songs With a Broken Heart

I'm so sick
Of listening
To love songs
With a broken heart

Sad Truths

I will look
For pieces of you
In everyone
Who comes after you

Inescapable Heartbreak

You can run away
From your city
And go
Somewhere new

But you can't run away
From how you feel.

Cruel Fantasy

Look up at the stars

I can see us

Together

Cruel fantasy.

Losing You

I've survived
Hard times
But nothing
Has been as hard
As losing you

Alone

Does anyone understand
How I feel?

Am I shouting
Into a void,
Hearing echoes
And mistaking them
For understanding?

Perhaps I am more alone
Than I thought.

<u>Chapter Three</u>

The Agony of Healing

The Agony of Healing

The agony of healing
Is the pain
Of the Phoenix
Going through the fire

Butterflies

I wonder
If it hurts
For caterpillars
To change into butterflies
In their cocoons

The same way it hurts
For a broken heart
To heal
And emerge
All the more beautiful
Than before

Poetry

Poetry
Is how we express
The inexpressible

Creators

We are
The creators
Of culture
Who dream the dreams
Of a generation

No Matter

You are beautiful
No matter your size
Your skin
Your hair
No matter what
You're beautiful

Never forget that

PC Language

Legislating morality
Is just as bad
When it comes from the left
As when it comes from the
right.

Fresh Start

I want to burn my life down
Throw everything out
Move cities
Change it all

I want
A fresh start

Crying

I wonder
If you cried over me
The way
I cried
Over you

More

I'm looking for more.

I want more out of life

I'm sick of settling

I'm sick of accepting
mediocrity

I want

More.

L. V.

Dear god
Heal
This broken
World

Violence is everywhere
People are dying

Dear god
What have we done

Respect

Never choose a man
Who doesn't respect his mother

If he doesn't respect
The woman
Who gave him life

How do you expect him
To respect you?

Cursed Wells

Loving you
Was a cursed well
Of endless despair

Weighted Chains

We are both
Weighed down
By demons of the past

How can we love each other
When it's so hard
To love
Ourselves

Mary

It's so sickening
That our country
Throws people in jail
For growing a leaf.

Declarations

Write me a song
Declare your love
Break down my walls
I'm crying for help
Help me
Heal
Myself

Tragic Knowledge

I was never enough for you
And I have
To come to terms
With that tragic fact

Live While You Can

Life is far too short
To care too much
About small things
That bother you

Life is too short
To be petty or cruel

Live while you can.

Signs

If you're looking
For a sign
To make that change
In your life

This is it.

Humankind

We can chop down forests
But not build schools
Because our priorities
Are fucked.

Ordinary People

Lovers aren't
Angels or demons

We are all people
Just trying our best

And that's
What's so hard about it all

Equal Rights

Love is love
Is love
Is love
Is love
Is love
Is love

<u>You</u>

Don't forget
Who you are

You are powerful
You are a goddess
You are beautiful

You
Are everything
you need

Why Can't We

Why can't we all
Just be
A little kinder
To one another?

What's so hard
About treating others
With basic respect
And human dignity?

How far we've fallen.

Slut

Women
Who enjoy sex
Shouldn't be labeled
As sluts

End of story.

Treat You Right

You deserve someone
Who wants to stay
Of their own will
Someone
Who you don't have to make
Treat you right

Slow Victory

I woke up this morning
Finally realizing
You weren't the last thought
I had thought
The previous night
And you weren't
The first thought
Of the morning

At last
Your grip
Had begun to loosen
On my fragile heart

Chapter Four

The Joy of Rebirth

The Joy of Rebirth

Today I woke up
Feeling like a new woman
Casting aside the shackles
Of loss and heartbreak

Here I am
Willing
To try again
At last, in the first stages
Of healing.

Symphony No. 9 – Mvt. No. 4

Nothing will ever
Be as beautiful
As the sweeping strings
Of Beethoven's ninth

What a shame
That classical music
Is dying out

You haven't really lived
Until you've cried
Over a violin's melody

91

Pillow Talk

I'm high on your words
Drunk on the promise
Of being yours
Tonight

For and By The People

Government for the people
By the people
Should look like its people

Too many rich white men
In power

There is still much change
Needed
To fight for

It Will All Work Out

You're gonna pass that test
That boy you like
Will ask you out
One day you'll have life
All figured out

Don't worry about it all
Right now

It'll all work out
Somehow, someday

Music of Love

How beautiful it is
To be so close to someone
That you know
The shape of their soul
And the music
Of their heartstrings

Family

Never forget you family.

Whether by blood
Or by choice
These people
Who are with you
Through it all
Must always be remembered
And loved.

Eulogy

Call your mother
While you still have the
chance
While she's still
On this earth

You'll never realize
How much she means to you
Until she's gone.

Moonlit Romance

Bring your lips
A little closer to mine

Let's fall in love
Under the stars
Warm coffee in hand

Kiss me
In the moonlight

Fall in love
With me.

It Starts With One Person

Spread some positivity today.

Tell your friends
You love them
Give a stranger
A compliment

Put some light
Into the world
Today.

It starts with one person.

By The Sea

Let's make out
By the sea
Listening to the waves crash
As we tell each other
Our deepest secrets
Let's watch the trees waver
In the gentle breeze
And take fistfuls of sand
In our hands
Making shapes as we please

Let's make out
By the sea

<u>x4</u>

It may be naive
But I believe
There is good
In every person

To Love a Soul

Everyone has a story
Everyone has a secret
Everyone has a past

To love these things
Is to love a soul

Flame

Lighters flicker
Beneath the stars
You and I
Sharing secrets

<u>Fragments</u>

Despondent christmases
Drunken mornings
Glasses empty

Search

Search for truth.

If nothing else
Try
To seek the truth
In everything.

Essential Experiences

There is nothing close
To the magic
Of hearing music live

Success

There is something beautiful
About the fact
That if I am successful
If this book is to be popular
It comes from you, the reader
and your support..

I cannot thank you enough.

-Adeline Whitmore

if you liked this book
please share it
review it
post about it
and spread the word

Made in the USA
San Bernardino, CA
27 March 2018